every grain of sand

a collection of poems and stories

JUSTIN SCRIBNER

Copyright © 2020 by Justin Scribner

All rights reserved. No part of this publication may be reproduced, distributed, or transmitted in any form by any means, including photocopying, recording, or other electronic methods without the prior written permission of the author, except in the case of brief quotations embodied in reviews and certain other noncommercial uses permitted by copyright law. For permission requests, write to the author at the address below.

jscribs@gmail.com

Illustrations by Lindsey Heddleston

ISBN: 978-0-578-77780-1

Printed in the United States of America.

First Printing, 2020.

For those who encourage and love unconditionally,
and through their simple generosity of spirit,
affect great change.

For Artie.

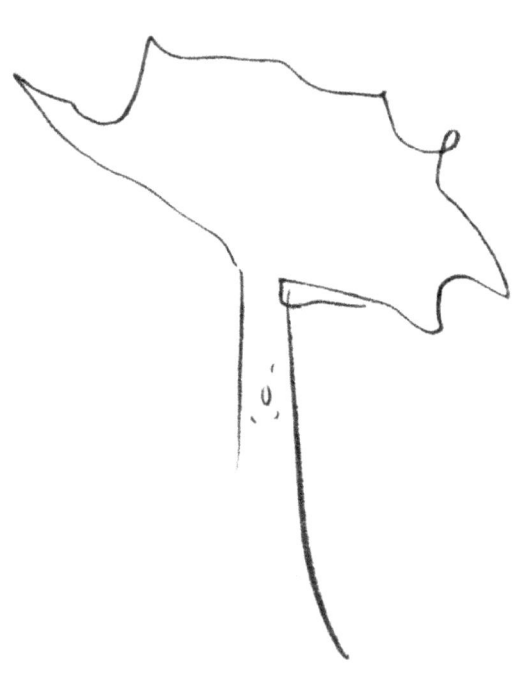

CONTENTS

Preface ix

Part One: Poems

too-sweet cotton candy	1
the age of the river	2
regression	3
yes, and	4
rowboat	5
the lightness of effort	6
the microscope and the moon	7
discarded	8
how he died in the very deep ocean	9
solitude	10
peephole	11
4:37	12
deconstruction	13
following the pattern	14
secret in his pocket	15
amor perezoso	16
as a bookmark	17
question your direction	18
as the end approached	19
xvi. the tower	20
kitchen sinking	21
crisp	22
our hole	23
losing herself in the celebration	24
murphy	25
spit it out	26
the boys	27
high pitches of expectation	28
Ticking All the Boxes	29
Out the Window	33
Upholstery	36

Floating	38
that's enough	39
Precipice	40
Released	42
woven	44
jigsaw	45
Blasphemy	46
Postcard from Springfield	47
Things to Do While Waiting for the Train	48
We Now Live in a Nature Preserve	49
Whale Song	50

Part Two: Stories

Bedtime Story	55
The Key	59
Lingering	63
Franchise	65
Blind Spot	67
Volcano	71
Theo	73
The Cindy	77

Part Three: Haiku

every grain of sand	89
Maple	90
sip my words slowly	92
knowing she'll be late	92
on a grassy square	93
you are a guitar	93
the space you gave me	94
you might as well be	94
peaches become ripe	94
a single finger	95
sanctify a touch	95
mother calmly sits	96

sometimes when you feel	96
the rhumba rhythms	96
whipped and flung sideways	97
a tree grips tightly	97
time has changed nothing	97
who are you? who now?	98
stopped along the walk	98
it doesn't take much	98
hospice	99
blessing for your trip	101
Gratitude	103

PREFACE

Why this book? Why now?

For my entire life, I have been a secret writer. I've filled notebooks with thoughts, ideas, stories, and hundreds of poems, hiding them in boxes, in attics, in basements. I dreamed of publishing them but often slid them into a drawer with a promise of *later, not yet.* It took a quarantine for me to realize, feeling purposeless and frustrated at home, that this moment is a gift, one I've been waiting on for decades. I'm finally making good on the promise to one day edit my short works into a compilation, joyfully closing a loop for myself. *Later is now.*

Though writing patiently rode in the backseat of my life, it is one of my first loves. I wrote my first-grade class play, an adaptation of a children's book about a Mexican volcano. In third grade, I worked for months on an episodic story about a boy who turned everything he touched into chocolate—a *delicious,* cautionary, Midas-inspired morality tale. Not long after, I saw a children's theater production of *Cinderella* and ran home to my mother's electric typewriter to render my own modern interpretation of the script. Then, in high school, I fell head-over-heels in love with poetry. I adored my creative writing teachers and idolized my peers who would fearlessly read their works to the class. They encouraged my attempts at sardonic, meditative observations of our wildly theatrical relationship struggles.

As my writing evolved over the past few decades, I found inspiration in the great Kurt Vonnegut, the deeply personal verse of Frank O'Hara, the unapologetic Charles Bukowski, the eccentric eloquence of Miranda July, the wry social commentary of George Saunders's short stories, the insightful and kooky quotidian microfiction of Lydia Davis, the wise and poignant poetry of Mary Oliver and Thich Naht Hanh, and the beautiful, haunting mysteries of Zen Buddhist koans.

This collection is organized into three parts: poems, short stories, and haiku. My haiku observe the traditional three-line format of seventeen syllables, arranged in a 5-7-5 pattern, but sometimes push other definitional boundaries of the genre, such as linking multiple stanzas. Typically, haiku examine an objective experience of a singular moment of nature, their brevity lending a sense of essentialism to everyday experiences. Haiku have always spoken to me as an outdoorsy meditator with a yen for wordplay, but I particularly resonate with one offshoot known as *senryū* poems, which lean into more cynical, human experiences.

Each section of this book is compiled in chronological order (with a few cheeky exceptions), from pieces written in high school to poems I wrote last month. The capitalization in the collection relates directly to when each piece was conceived. Everything written before my 31st birthday is almost entirely lowercase, including pronouns. Around New Year's of 2012, something changed. I couldn't tell while it was happening, but it was a maturing, a spiritual growth spurt. I began to see myself and the world differently and writing the lowercase "i" was no longer possible for me. I decided to write more story-driven works using proper capitalization and punctuation. The Preface and Dedication were written recently, so the capitalization is standard, but the dream of a collection was one from my twenties, therefore, the book title "every grain of sand" is all lowercase.

I am inclined towards books, poems, stories, and plays that offer provocative questions in everyday situations and conjure remarkable ways of feeling, seeing, or thinking that shake me out of old patterns and perspectives. My hope is that something in this collection inspires you, provokes you, provides you some comfort. May a word, phrase, or idea ignite something in you—and through the power and promise of those small fires in each of us, may we be encouraged to live with blazing passion and staggering compassion.

PART ONE
–
POEMS

TOO-SWEET COTTON CANDY

like an untamed tiger,
an uncontrollable sneeze,
a raging wave,
my curious heart
impulsively sneaks off
without me
to the carnival
in the town by the beach,
riding the ferris wheel,
getting sunburnt,
wolfing down treat
after treat,
ping-ing from
one impossible
fluorescent game
to another

and here i sit—
a stuffed animal
waiting to be won

4th February 1997

THE AGE OF THE RIVER

time is an illusion, they say,
    and though you can count the days
        since the ferns began to grow,
and you can track the times
    that the water has frozen over
        since your childhood,

and each tree that watches from overhead,
    casting glorious, shadowed
        lacework on the rocks,
could reveal a number of rings by which
    you could count how many seasons
        the lace has been cast,

the river is only the sum of its parts,
    so it's more accurate to say
        that *it* really has no age,
its well-worn banks lined
    with countless grains of sand
        infinitesimal,

each immigrated from beyond
    here for maybe a century,
        here maybe just for now,
and the water, ah,
    the water is fresh every second
        and impossible to quantify,

flowing through, tumbling forward,
    flying past, around this thing
        we call *the river,*
every eyeblink its contents replenished
    in one minute   all new water
        in one hundred years   all new people.

                30th April 2020

REGRESSION

i need to move backward into my niche
from before. my current surroundings
cannot protect like that snug suite
of security, my warm bed before
dreaming where gravity had no
pull, where i floated like a fish,
the soft space where love was
the liquid that never ran dry
where i simply ate through
my belly, before air and
grief came in the same
breath . . . to regress
back to the time
before worries,
before cares,
before
me.

21st February 1997

YES, AND

for each beginning there's a death in refusal
and for each ending a contradiction
between one's unconditional love
and the doubt of possibilities that exist

if negativity proves that no seeds
sown to rock grow tall enough to be proud,
then the lonely pessimist must remember that
ideas born out of awe weigh the least

15th July 2005

ROWBOAT

i dream myself to the center
of a lake i've never touched
and the image trickles clear:

a simple dock ahead,
water's face almost still,
sky as empty as a clean plate waiting.

my bare feet flat on the bottom boards,
my seat warm from the sun,
the wood soft and worn,

a comforting slow lilt,
drifting towards shade.
no room for petty ambitions,

my fingers trace the edges
of the tired oar handles
along forest green paint crackles,

my hands
so gratefully
empty.

22nd July 2005

THE LIGHTNESS OF EFFORT

the worker bee
does not question
her superiors,
does not dominate
the conveyor belt
with non sequiturs
alluding to inane
virile uniqueness.

the hive's anonymity
allows the bee
to simply address
the workload—
stitch by stitch—
providing
plenty of time
to daydream
about roses
and honey.

28th July 2005

THE MICROSCOPE AND THE MOON

i'm a bug on a leaf, one of zillions
looking up through massive, rolling clouds,
thinking i can conquer the moon.

inspect a scale view blueprint of my building
and you'll encounter hundreds of rooms, compartments
filled with colorful junk and empty memorabilia.

dissect my mind into parts with the humdrum enthusiasm
of a biologist researching the exoskeleton of a bug corpse,
endless wrinkles and folds, a zillion unspecial pixels.

a microscope can't determine what actually
keeps me ticking and no lens can define
how much of the moon can fit in my pocket.

20th September 2005

DISCARDED

the moment
you set me down,
so distracted,
the air whistled through
the crack in the door.

deserted
three years
in the same position,
my pages longing,
yellowed.

re-read me, please.
thaw my brittle fingers,
i can't wait to feel you with them.
if you crack my spine,
i will touch you back.

15th December 2005

HOW HE DIED IN THE VERY DEEP OCEAN

counting clouds as his rosary,
he had been treading water
methodically since morning.
as it slowly grew darker,
he could sense it coming.
with only twenty-two seconds
left before he sank,
his toes curled down,
his thighs froze up,
a shooting charley horse,
a stiff foot arched,
a cement right leg,

and his left arm flailed,
and the other grabbed his calf,
and his neck tilted back,
and his jaw became the
mouth of a salt river that
swiftly overwhelmed him.

the warm memory of
a beautiful something
passed through,
but it was also gone—
a fleeting moment lost.

28th December 2005

SOLITUDE

i anticipated moments of meditation,
times when i would need space away
from all of you. i always assumed i
would be able to control when that
would be and how long it would
last—but never considered that
being away from others is not
the same as being with myself.

even though they told me,
"you are your own best friend,"
i didn't face it eye to eye
until i was there, alone:
talking quietly in circles,
devouring word puzzles,
navigating the difference
between lonely and alone.

7th February 2006

PEEPHOLE

the family's shiny brown camaro
developed a surprising flaw
through a decade of weathering.

you couldn't see it from the outside,
nor could you tell from the way it drove
(the smooth ride satisfied the father)

but as passengers pulled up the stained, khaki car mat
at their feet, they exposed a small hole,
and the road whizzed quickly beneath them.

it wasn't even as wide as a quarter at first,
but after only a year the eldest son could fit
his hand all the way through the rusty aperture.

the father kept it from the mother, his pride.
the eldest son kept it from his brother, a secret,
and, driving to tee-ball practice with his father,

he snuck the mat aside with his sneaker,
imagining sliding his leg through the hole slowly,
shaving it off into the churning gravel underneath.

10th February 2006

4:37

it could've been any 4:37 in the last three days
and, since i was out of town when it happened,
no one was there to see the hands stop moving.

seeing the second hand frozen, i sense
all of the other things that must have stopped
in the last three days:

the batteries that failed,
and the people who expired,
and the relationships that ended,

and what a surprise it must've been to those unlucky onlookers,
adjusting, like i must now, to not having a clock.
if not a clock, adjusting to change.

15th June 2006

DECONSTRUCTION

while the edifice of you and i
was being built, you left
our windows open,
not just cracked,
gaped wide all day—
letting in dirt,
letting out smells—
left that way for weeks.

you never shut them,
i felt welcome.
next door the Chinese men
alternated between drilling
and pouring cement.
we took turns with
brick and mortar too,
but even with the fresh air
passing through the room,
you became clammy,
constrained by
unconscious fears.

when you asked nicely
to close the windows,
i couldn't grasp the
gravity of your request.
its significance was lost
in the breeze above
the construction site
while we deconstructed.

18th June 2006

FOLLOWING THE PATTERN

when you are counting
the days since
he called you,
you are counting.

when you loop yarn
through aluminum
needles, under,
around, and off,
you are knitting.

the boiling pot
continues singing,
and i am knitting,
not counting.

                        20th June 2006

SECRET IN HIS POCKET

he kept his hand a secret.
he walked with it
in his pocket

only making reference
to it once a year.

when someone asked,
he would retort that they
had "no right to pry"
or they were "just jealous,"
but really, he was
afraid someone wanted
to take his hand,
and then he wouldn't
have one at all.

                                           7th August 2006

AMOR PEREZOSO

su cara sudorosa,
mi mano pegajosa,
las dos mantas se tocan
en media sombra cerca de un gran roble.

nada se mueve hoy
con excepción de las nubes
y somos los únicos que las miran
rodar y rodar y rodar.

mi mano pegajosa que limpia
su frente sudorosa,
mis expectativas perdieron
en la meditación
de dos personas superpuestas
en dos mantas.

                        1st August 2006

LAZY LOVE

his face is sweaty,
my hand is sticky,
the two blankets are touching
in half-shade near a wide oak.

nothing moves today
except for the clouds
and we are the only ones
who watch them
roll and roll and roll.

my sticky hand cleans
his sweaty forehead,
my expectations lost
in the meditation
of two people overlapping
on two blankets.

AS A BOOKMARK

hurry—her tea kettle whistled
she ran to turn off the stereo—
spun scarf around neck—
poured green tea into thermos—
grabbed new planner—pen—
highlighter—old college prep book—
flung open front door—
whole morning crashed down

hot tea splashed against hardwood
as the book fell open to page 231
and a glossy Kodak print
stored away as a bookmark years ago
slid underneath the console table.
she squatted with a groan,
holding her scarf out of the puddle
to pull the photo into the light:

the image of a joyful family,
dinner scene long buried,
a young, simple life,
a nuclear foursome
engaged in separate schemes
that would tear them
into unrelated futures—

safely returned to page 231

                      21st September 2006

QUESTION YOUR DIRECTION

if given the choice between
a difficult trail to climb,
maneuvering prickly brush,
muscling against gravity,
and a pastoral hill to
safely stroll down,

consider taking
the challenge over the ride
because after the sweat,
the tears, and the strain,
you're on top of the mountain.
and oh, the view.

9th October 2006

AS THE END APPROACHED

with a grimace,
he spat onto the linoleum—
the conversation was over
and nothing was left.
across the kitchen island, deflated,
she wrapped herself tighter
into his still damp, blue polyester blazer.

he heard his next wife
singing a decade away.
when he reached for his jacket,
she grabbed his left arm,
"don't leave me until i've
read the last chapter!"

he yanked his blazer away
and tossed her the whole book,
which fluttered into the fountain—
woosh—and the ink dissolved,
fouling their small pond with a
black cloud that would stain.

                              14th October 2006

XVI. THE TOWER

drenched onlookers
across from an apartment fire
under a grey awning

with restless jaws agape
rub up against each other
and their soaked umbrellas

bricks careen to the sidewalk
the audience gasps
the wood sighs and cracks

sour flames reach to the pelting storm
while the embers surrender in pops
fizzling into hot puddles

murmurs of regret float
like ashen flakes of paper
raining all around

                                    3rd December 2006

KITCHEN SINKING

mother has been pressed into a tirade,
her tears stream down the walls
and doorways as she wails, leaving
water stains on the walnut cabinets
and a dirty ring around
the waist of the kitchen while

her son vacillates
between focused concern and
wild, uncompromising self-interest,
both drowning in their arguments,
flailing, reaching for something
secure to float on while they scream.

father has learned not to hear
the high-pitched tones in their voices,
not exactly deaf, but also partly blind,
eating a side of scrambled eggs,
no salt, no butter on his toast
and, even though it's burnt,

he doesn't send it back,
no substitutions.
he meekly sulks off,
leaving his empty dishes
on the table for the two
angry waitstaff to break.

6th December 2006

CRISP

the skies in such sharp focus
the clouds so well defined
drawn with care
unparalleled attention

no leaf un-veined or reflection forgotten
the movement of wind captured
by every piece of clothing
slow-moving pedestrians wear

a clear whisper of squirrel sounds
each tree placed neatly apart
shadows falling identically
dimension and perspective aligned

the heart of a crisp moment
intangible   captured
just as the chill in the air
lingers like a first kiss

12th December 2006

OUR HOLE

between the couch
and the television,
an impeding hole
sunk dead center
in the small room
made it difficult to
steer around the
apartment easily.

we endured months,
keenly aware of the
unspoken danger,
never moving
too quickly,
desperate to ignore it,
before we were both
swallowed whole.

27th March 2007

LOSING HERSELF IN THE CELEBRATION

a soft reverie playing
with loose, heavy hands

the beat drifting *legato* dizzy
lamps reflecting sloshing martinis

and eyeglasses catching glimpses
flashes of light mimicking

the tinkling soprano tings
of the higher octaves

with the champagne
tickles going down.

                                        30th March 2007

MURPHY

    make the bed

    make your bed

        lie in it

            deal with it

  fold it up

square folds

    put it away

          think it over

         sleep it off

    make the bed

             3rd July 2008

SPIT IT OUT

sticking
to   the roof of her mouth
words wrap   a round   each   oth er
she tries   to   lick   them out

a peanut butter sandwich apology
that   stays   with her
the rest of the day.

25th August 2008

THE BOYS

around the Village around Hell's Kitchen
at the stools at the bars despite
the weather despite each other
on the subway on ecstasy into
the streets into the trains
between martinis between clubs
below 14th street below the belt
beneath neon lights beneath one another
against rails against their word
inside backrooms inside each other
until someone stops them until never

19th October 2009

HIGH PITCHES OF EXPECTATION

we say without a doubt that the sun will rise,
but somehow that truth doesn't comfort.
we rely on the tides,
circularities that keep tires rolling.
our can-do will-do cheer
is based on that expectation:
things that die, grow.
things that leave, return.

the earth certainly bounces back,
tirelessly repeating itself,
much like our unrelenting
sunny dispositions.
the world turns and turns,
plowing over speculation:
things that grow, die.
things that come, go.

our neighbors cling
to their glossy faith
that they deserve mercy
from the pelting rain,
clutching histories
and anticipating results,
overestimating themselves,
too cocky for umbrellas.

it's no wonder we put the
blame outward and expect
the answer to come from within.
we pray for revolution
even though everyone knows
rain doesn't fall upwards.

24th August 2010

TICKING ALL THE BOXES

I must remember to vacuum this afternoon,
Kath thought proudly. No one kept house
like the women in her family. It was in their blood.

She lifted the corner of the rigid mattress
and tucked the pale blue flat sheet under carefully,
folding in one side, then the other,

hospital style, as her mother taught her.
Kath smiled at her work and felt complete.
Thirty-nine years old and still patting herself on the back

when she completed those simple tasks
her mother would have approved of.
Not appreciated, but expected.

It was clear where her perfectionism came from.
The impact of her mother's apprehensive love
reverberating through her every move.

Her younger sister Lara hadn't inherited
their family's organizational impulses
and their mother always felt that was a shame.

Someday, I'll help get her things in order,
she thought. Lara would really benefit
from a good closet redesign, for starters.

That would be a lovely Christmas gift this year.
I wish Lara were as generous as I am.
She can be a lost cause, can't she?

Shoot. Kath grimaced as she realized
how late in the morning it was already.
No time to vacuum. I'll do it tomorrow.

I thought I had time today. Where did those
three hours go? Ah, well. No one's perfect.
I should also buy new dishtowels soon

and do something about my rough elbows.
Why do I always have so much to do?
Oh well. No guests this month,

at least. There hadn't been
a visitor for about six months,
when her sorority sister's niece, Madison,

stayed with her for two nights
while interviewing for a job.
Kath took exemplary care of her.

Maddy didn't get the job. I shouldn't
keep a nice home just for guests, I should
do it for myself. Eat off of my good china.

What's the use in saving them for special
moments, especially when those rarely
come? Maybe I'll buy pink towels this

time. Or green. That would match nicely.
I like light greens—they are clean
and show that I have a sense of whimsy.

A horn sounded on the street
outside, crass and sudden,
for a beat too long.

Some people have no respect for aural space.
What was so important
that they had to lay on the horn so hard?

It was a quiet residential
street, for Christ's sake. She felt a burp
inside her chest, drifting upwards.

She quickly found her coffee mug and took
a sip, swallowing slowly and deliberately.
That's better.

She began to pick out the right shoes
to wear, but none of the ones
she owned were very nice anymore.

A perfect metaphor for my life, Kath chuckled.
Out-of-style, worn-in, and a few years too old.
She selected her least comfortable pair,

burgundy slip-ons that matched a nice,
warm cardigan she inherited last month
from her sweet, but overweight, friend Dee.

She was going to see Dee at a birthday
party that evening and wanted her
to know how much she appreciated

her generosity. And also show her
how good the sweater looked hanging
from her far more diminutive frame.

Keys? Yes. Phone? Yes. Wallet? Yes.
Eyes done? Yes. Lipstick? Yes. Hair . . . ?
A quick look at the mirror before recoiling

and laughing to herself at her own horror.
Dee is going to comment on my roots,
I just know it. She's always razzing me about

my hair styles. I should put it up. I will.
Kath dug in her side drawer for a clip.
She expertly twisted her hair up,

sweeping up the side pieces, clipping them
in a little higher than usual.
The height suits me, she thought.

I could do that now and then on days when
I feel bloated. Yes, it actually lengthens me.
Dee will like it, I'm sure.

After all, her hair is so fine, she wouldn't
look this good with it in a clip. I'll keep it.
The updo made her look older and she knew it.

It wasn't worth fighting anymore.
She briskly grabbed her purse and headed
across the oriental rug for the front door.

Oh, my mug! I hate coming home to dishes.
She quickly scrubbed it down and rinsed it out,
stopping to evaluate her cuticles.

It's just a frustrating cycle of constant
evaluation and upkeep, she mused.
I'm never ever done, am I?
Nothing's ever really perfect, is it?

                          1st August 2012

OUT THE WINDOW

Fiore huddles in his mother's puffy jacket
on the upholstered bench next to the cold window.
The air conditioners are on high as usual
and the fan points towards him while he reads
his assigned pages, but it looks warm outside.
He takes a break from social studies
to finally watch the children whose voices
had been dancing around his textbooks.
He grips the fleece edges of the coat,
assessing the neighborhood kids
in shorts and t-shirts and bright sneakers
playing stickball on the stoop
diagonally across the street.

There's Evan and his sister—I forget her name.
Evan looks like he's winning, his smile is so wide.
That boy from Willow Street is definitely not winning.
He's always on this block playing with the kids
but never really seems happy about it.
I wonder why he even comes around.
I wonder what his name is?
He looks about nine, but I bet he'd beat me
if I went out there to join them.
Maybe he just needs to win a game or two.
Then maybe he'd smile. . . .

I would go out and watch from my tree
for a while before Evan would say
Hi Fiore! Do you wanna play too?
I would smile kindly and shake my head no
and his sister would come to grab my pant leg
so I acquiesce, sheepishly.

They hand me the ball to throw.
Even though they expect me to sink
the ball into Mr. Parry's yard by accident,
I aim carefully and pitch like a professional.
That's all that the boy from Willow Street needs,
a good, solid pitch. He creams the ball,
sending it reeling all the way down the block.
The surprise of his success beams across his face
and he looks at me and laughs *Thank You* sarcastically.
I fake my upset that he's done so well,
but deep down I know I just earned everyone's respect.
Fiore is actually a pretty good pitcher, Evan says,
and his sister taps me like she wants an autograph
and asks me if I've ever played before
and why I don't come out more often
and do I want to come inside and see their playroom.
I just shrug her off like the other boys do,
but. . . .

Oh, they are going inside now.
I guess Evan finally won.
The boy from Willow Street is picking
up his backpack and waving goodbye.
Evan's sister tries to start another game,
but Evan shoos her away and sits between
the houses with some of his cool little cars.
She feels my gaze and quickly looks up at me,
wondering who I am. She tilts her head a little
and her eyes ask too many questions.

Don't ask me why I don't come out.
Don't ask me why I'm not good at sports.

Don't ask me what my name is.
Don't ask me why I'm not doing my homework.
Don't ask me to be your friend. I'm not allowed.

Fiore sneers at her, even though he doesn't mean to.
She checks windows for adult faces
and then, setting her hands on her hips,
she firmly sticks her tongue out and
thrusts her middle finger up to him.
Fiore jumps off the window seat
and zips up his mother's coat.
God, I hate kids.

                              6th August 2012

UPHOLSTERY

The pops of color in the upholstery
evenly mirrored her thoughts.
She sat on them, leaned on them,
stared at the little squares, fixated.

The burnt red was her husband
whom she loved but had been avoiding recently,
knowing that in their next conversation
she would somehow find a way to complain
about the weekends in her passive-aggressive way,
about his unattractive lazing around
in basketball shorts playing solitaire on his iPad.

The dark teal squares were her deep-seated fear
of losing her job, which seemed inevitable
at the rate her boss was budgeting their department
and the depth to which her heart sank
sitting at her desk each morning,
daydreaming through her Amazon Wishlist.

The drab orange was the incessant anger
that she should have demanded she finish
her graduate degree before having children
and that she may never get back to it.

The pale green was her favorite TV in the kitchen
which was hers—and hers only—after bedtime,
the only respite in her week,
besides the twenty minutes she allowed herself
for coffee each morning at work at 9:10 a.m.
and that was really a chocolate brown square.

The sky blue was her upsetting intuition
that her brother might pass soon.
She sensed it every time there was a cloudless sky,
every time she let her glass of water slow to stillness,
every time the world seemed to pause.
She knew he didn't have long and there would be
a quietness in that part of her busy mind.

The heather grey squares were her to-do list,
a constant fuzzy noise pervading
all of her moments in transit and permeating
the in-between times of talking with coworkers.

The light tan was her little girl
who she knew would grow up to dislike her
and always say, "Thanks a lot, Jackie."
"Thanks for showing me how not to do everything,"
her familiar sarcasm coating the truth
that they were no different from each other,
twins born twenty-six years apart
and both sinking in quicksand,
hot with the vitriol of their own design.

She pushed off of the couch to sit in the other room
where the wooden seats were not her feelings.

11th August 2012

FLOATING

Keep my feet outstretched, leading the way,
center engaged, arms at my sides, a fine
balance of relaxed and aware, trusting
and ready, willing and prepared, breathing
slowly, faith in the water. Bobbing on my
back, coasting comfortably, I know
the rules for floating. A few turns
full of confidence—but is that a
waterfall gush down the channel? I'll
swim off before the edge pulls me
over—but it will be too late, I'll
flounder. No, I'll just release
the struggle, roll supine, drift over
the falls, plunge, bob up, find my bearings,
and drift on. And if it becomes
too shallow, I'll sit up and
ford the slippery sandbar until
the river deepens.
                      Are the stiller
waters the time to stretch your legs
and recommit to the twists and turns
ahead? I hear it's miles and miles
of this, but I know this river
is going somewhere. And really,
finding that somewhere is why
I'm floating in the first place.

21st August 2012

THAT'S ENOUGH

we sabotage ourselves
so that people will see
that we are flawed

so people will depend on us less

so people won't expect as much

so people might think twice
before relying on us again.

                              28th August 2012

PRECIPICE

The breeze nearly knocked me over
that night. I was so light—and ready to go.
Looking down at the moon's reflection
in the canal below made me dizzy.
My heart was heavier than ever,
I was top-heavy and listing.

The city spanned the horizon beyond,
while the rippling water and the cars
zooming across the bridge behind me,
noses up, ignoring me, were as waves,
rocking me side-to-side,
an undertow rhythm,
pushing me to jump,
pulling me to the street.

"Take a fall, plunge quickly,"
the breeze smiled, gently
nudging me like I was an infant
on a playground swing.
I could go over at any second.
I gripped the bannister and
steadied my sloshy brain.
What was I thinking?
How could I consider this?
The breeze whispered
across the back of my neck,
lifting my hair up, urging.

I could see the escape button.
I could almost touch the relief.

I could end it so effortlessly,
the universe almost asking me to.
But my backpack.
But my shoes.
But the bannister.
But the bystanders.
But the heartache mourning.
But the future.
But the moon. . . .

Calmly taking my chin and
lifting my gaze, she said,
"I know how you feel.
It takes everything in me
not to jump each night."

And the moon has kept me
alive every night since.

                        4th September 2012

RELEASED

It's not the grand unlatching
of a series of locks and gadgets
that you expected.

Click.

The door gently swings open—and that's it—
no small band playing, no crowd of loving family
and friends from every year of life
emerging into a thousand weepy hugs.
Instead, it is raining and there is
a single person standing just down
the entryway by a taxicab.

The raindrops are so fine that they float
and not always straight down,
sometimes sideways, so it's almost misting,
which gives you permission to well up
at this miraculous moment.
Hearing that click unleashes
a furious relief inside you
and tears finally start rolling.

You wrap your arms around your bag
as you walk to the cab but
being a free man all of a sudden
makes you feel heavy, each step
more difficult than the last.
You're not skipping out triumphantly,
singing and cheering like you predicted.

You pause, magnetically drawn
backwards toward your prison.
You already miss it,
your friends, your cell,
your seat in the cafeteria,
your bench in the yard,
your thinking spot in the workroom.
It's all over. It's all over.
It's all over.

                        10th October 2012

WOVEN

(for Sarita)

like a basket woven tight
with hay and sticks and string,
our friendship has been
cobbled together by
all sorts of experiences.

the vessel is strong
and holds so much love
that it takes two of us
to carry it down
to the village.

24th October 2012

JIGSAW

one can complete a thousand-piece puzzle
in the same way that a psychotherapist
connects dots with focused diligence
for a patient's diagnosis:

build a frame by finding edges first,
group pieces together by color, by type,
and place them in, piece by piece,
with a confident knowing
that the patient was born a whole person—
cracked into a thousand fragments by
cruel, confusing experiences
the world has tossed their way—
they are capable of being whole again,
just like a puzzle-maker knows that
a freshly opened jigsaw is
never missing any pieces.

13th November 2012

BLASPHEMY

Considering the amount of time spent instilling
traditional values like honor, trust, and integrity
in her students, she is flabbergasted

by the manifesto she discovers written across
her chalkboard in fine, black Sharpie. She sets down
purse and tote bag, heart thumping

out of her chest as she takes it all in. She doesn't even
want to read it, afraid that the venom behind the
perpetrator's graffiti might taste familiar.

She glances around the room for obvious clues to
who might have been there last and what time
they might have committed the vandalism.

She had been trying to go easier on them since
reading their entries on ratemyteachers.com, but there
were students who still hated her and

passed notes saying as much—she even found
one on the floor last month. *Ooh, I could
compare the handwriting!*

She pulls the tattered notepaper out of
the zipper pocket on the side of her purse
and unfolds the evidence. Holding it up

to the light between herself and the manifesto,
she feels a surprising excitement from this
blasphemous act of rebellion—and the fact that

she is the lucky target.

27th June 2013

POSTCARD FROM SPRINGFIELD

What a lovely surprise it was this gloomy afternoon
to receive your postcard. It seemed like junk mail

at first—I assumed it was from a dentist or chiropractor,
an appointment reminder. But then I saw the image—

the cat in a hammock—and I laughed. You got me! I'm
relieved you liked your hotel room in Springfield

and family was getting along, despite the circumstances. I'm
glad you found time to write me, although there was

plenty of time, I'm sure. It was nice, is what I'm
saying, that you chose to spend the quiet moments

between the funeral and the family meals to send me
that goofy cat in sunglasses. I'm sure it helped to

lighten the mood for you, too, while sorting through the
layers of mourning. I'm honored you chose me and I'll

cherish the cat, knowing that even during Sidney's
passing, you had the foresight to send your future self

a laugh in the mail, a reminder that life moves on.

28th March 2015

THINGS TO DO WHILE WAITING FOR THE TRAIN

Look up the track.

Look at the time, add the minutes.
Half-smile, scooting out of the way politely.

Look up the track, calculate the time a taxi would take,
contemplate the cost of a taxi, resolve to be late again.

Weigh the pros and cons of owning a bicycle.
Imagine the horror of a gruesome bicycle accident.

Look at the time, look up the track.
Look down the track, just in case.

Force an inhale as deep as you can,
one breath closer.

Locate the wooden bench down the way.
Notice the growing number of people waiting.

Admire their shoes, take mental stock of your
shoe collection, enumerating which you wear most often.

Compare your sneakers to others' around you.
Guess the price of the nicest pair you see.

Get out your phone to make a note
of the shoes you'd like for your birthday,

notice the time, add the minutes,
feel the heat of anxiety rushing to your ears.

Hear a train rumble, look up the track.

28th March 2015

WE NOW LIVE IN A NATURE PRESERVE

Just when our alarms once pierced the dawn,
the jubilant arias begin.

A choir of starlings warm up
near the recycling bins and low baritone

doves coo on a fire escape date. They see us
craning out of open windows,

peering into their nature preserve.
Melodies float through

where cacophonies—squealing, revving,
shouting, blaring—trampled

the breezes only two months ago.
The birds' up-tempo ballads fly, unfettered

by the pressures of productivity,
the transactions of worry,

the panic of the newest news.
Barbershop seagulls congregate calmly

on a bench near a family of sparrows,
debating harmonies on the street corner.

Immune to future-focused what-could-bes,
they take flight, echoing freedom

from brownstone to brownstone,
praising the cracked open skies.

3rd May 2020

WHALE SONG

Legends tell of ancient moaning,
distant low tones encoded
with Paleolithic stories,
obscured below the surface of my waking,
contrasted with imperceptibly high notes,
divinely poetic arias, above
the mindless chatter that reverberates
between the lines of everything I read.
Many listen for your songs
from little boats, ears pressed
to the great profound, waiting
for ballads to breach the mirror.
Do you sing to be loved?

I sift through history's rhythms
for your mammoth ocean melodies
and your warbling in the mountains,
where it's rumored you roamed
eons ago with other mammals.
Did you bellow your
whale song with words then?
How did you translate
your vast knowledge into
amniotic sound frequencies?

I ask earnestly, but don't
wait for your reply.
I want to face you, but
plug my ears to steer clear
of all beloved behemoths—
the legend of Moby Dick,

Pinocchio, and the mythical Jonah,
the Big Blue Room at the Museum,
the whale mural at Port Authority—
anything that might place me
squarely mid-ocean, floating
in the dark abyss alone,
squinting through deep waters.

For you, I'm not a threat,
an indistinct plankton.
For me, you are confrontation:
eyes to eye with a colossus,
with loss of control,
the fear of the unknown,
facing nothingness,
feeling small enough
to be swallowed whole.

It is no relief that I would hear
you approaching first. It is, in fact,
your breathtaking lullaby
that scares me, the terror
of our impending encounter,
of what could happen.

5th July 2020

PART TWO
–
STORIES

BEDTIME STORY

After the door shuts and the footsteps die, but long before their parents' voices fade completely, the two little boys sit up in their beds. The older one switches on his small yellow lamp and calls the younger one's name.

"I'm awake, are you? Wanna go look?" The younger one nods vigorously and smiles back, mischief and curiosity in their eyes. Where could their Christmas presents be hiding this year?

The older one pulls on his socks to help pad his footfalls on the sometimes-creaky floorboards. With calm precision, the younger one opens their bedroom door a crack and floods the room with light from the hallway. Even though they hear their mother's voice downstairs in the kitchen, they must make sure that their father isn't up here; they can't get caught. The older brother mimes that he'll play lookout, stepping quickly to the top of the stairs and planting himself on the carpet. He peeps down at the landing of the first floor where his mother's shadow flits back and forth, putting away clanging dishes.

The younger boy has made it to the hallway linen closet and already started scanning the lowest three shelves (the only ones he can reach). He pushes piles of sheets and towels aside, hoping to find toy cars or video games hidden in the back. He gives up on the taller shelves and closes the door in a demonstrative, but silent, show of frustration. He tiptoes to their father's office next, determined to find the secret spot.

The older brother has gotten comfortable on his stomach with his head propped up on his elbows, watching the mother's shadow confidently dance about as she tidies. He listens closely to her, straining to hear as much as he can of her conversation; she is not on the phone, as he first thought, but talking with his father, who replies now and then with a low laugh or murmur of approval. She's telling his father about a friend she saw for coffee and how his business is "just thriving." The boy can't make out every word but is able to follow her story about how her friend got a promotion and paid for their food and something about this almost bragging seems to be rubbing his father the wrong way by the sounds of his grunts and the tone of his questions.

"How did Mister Moneybags find time (garbled noise) so important?"

His mother's shadow stops, and she puts her hand on her hip.

"Don't get jealous."

The younger brother is done investigating the entire office closet, rummaging behind all of the boxes and papers. He turns his attention to the big wooden desk, knowing that there's a strong chance their gifts are stashed in the back of one of the half empty drawers. The left side has nothing special in it, so he turns to the ones on the right where he knows he will discover the gold.

The mother's shadow has stepped away from the doorway now, and the older boy has taken two steps closer to their conversation. He cranes his neck down, leaning on the bannister to hear better. It sounds like they've begun quarreling but are using more hushed tones. He hears pops of "trust" and "fucking disgusting" and "quiet, they're asleep" and "don't talk to me that way" and "never again" and "will you shut up about that?"

A chair screeches across the linoleum and hits the side of the counter.

The younger boy smiles as he pulls out the top drawer—this would be the perfect hiding spot for Nintendo boxes, just little enough to fit underneath his father's notepads. He lifts them up to reveal a dark brown cardboard container and a wide black box with white lettering.

Knowing that they aren't presents, he still pulls them out onto the floor. He lifts the brown one first, lighter than the other, and shakes it. There is a little tinkle of jewelry or coins. With a smile, he lifts off the lid. His eyes bulge out of their sockets seeing dozens of *real* shiny silver bullets all lined up. Panic-stricken, he immediately sets the top back on the box and slides it under the notepads.

He considers wiping the drawer down with his sleeve, but his father wouldn't fingerprint the room—he'll never know he's seen them. He runs out of the office full steam, heart beating out of his chest and into his ears, and bumps his brother's leg, which has been propped onto the top stair for leverage. The surprise almost knocks the older brother off-balance, and he juts his neck out to angrily mouth "What?" The younger brother almost points but decides he's better off not alarming him.

"Nothing. Come on, let's go back," he whispers. The older one doesn't want to; the fight is just getting good. He waves off his brother who runs into their room and under his covers.

"Now, don't!" the older boy hears. She begins to cry. They've stopped talking. His father's shadow comes into view, as wide and imposing as a bear. He stands still, looking to the side, presumably at his wife. The boy steps to the top stair and lies down again out of view, poking his head up just enough to see if he will hit her again. Even though it's just a shadow, he wants to see her get slapped, to be a witness, to see the proof for himself. A glass shatters and there's a muffled scream.

"Now look what you've done!" followed by muffled silence, like a sustain pedal.

Soon, shoes pound up the carpeted stairs. The older brother scampers back into his room and, gripping the doorknob, shuts the door without a noise. He hears his father go into the bathroom and run water. He knows that it's over for the night, and everything is fine now. His mother is downstairs picking the shards off of the floor, and soon his father will be in bed.

"You okay?" he says to his younger brother. "Why did you freak out?" The little one pretends to be asleep, grasping his penis with both hands to keep from peeing the bed again.

The older brother shuts off his lamp and slides back into bed, wondering which glass broke this time.

Outside, trees sway and the moonlight through the leaves casts a net of light on the wall across from the younger brother's bed. He tries to squeeze his legs together tighter as he watches the shadows breathe and drift from side to side. The bathroom door creaks open loudly in the hallway and the little boy gasps as warm urine spreads across his underwear and up his shirt.

30th August 2012

THE KEY

It was a day of struggle after struggle. First, her favorite blue umbrella snapped and folded inside out into the wind. Then, after running two blocks in her sandals through sideways rain to the closest F train stop, she discovered that all trains from Brooklyn were running express after 10 p.m. The stairs into the subway were blocked by a single pink piece of ribbon tied to each side rail.

With her shoulders hunched and eyes half-open, Annie scanned the buildings through her dripping wet bangs for a place to pull out her phone and text Jon. Now she was going to be even later than she'd thought for their date, rounding out her record of three dinners, three times late.

None of the entrances on the block had awnings. In fact, the wind was pelting fat raindrops into the glass doors. Across the street, there was a small deli that looked closed, a church with a massive set of stairs leading up to a stained-glass entrance, and a slightly crooked house on the corner with a porch covered in house plants and ivy.

A cyclist zoomed down the otherwise deserted street, little lights blinking white from his front handlebars. He had a handsome smile and broad shoulders—like Mike. He dinged his bell as he passed her in recognition of the terrible weather and Annie nodded back. She hadn't thought about Mike in weeks. She watched the cyclist pedal off into the storm, leaving a red streak across the wet street behind his blue shorts.

She glanced both ways and bolted across the intersection for the cute house on the corner. Sploosh! Her left foot sank down into a cold lake of dirty water in a long, deep pothole. Her toes scraped the side of the asphalt and she yelped, reaching down to pull her loose sandal back on. *Just my luck,* she thought. Was there a way to start this whole week over?

She sprinted onto the sidewalk and gingerly hopped up the two stairs onto the dry, wooden porch of the corner house. It was a huge relief to lift her head up and stretch her shoulders back. She wiped rain from her eyes, accidentally smearing mascara on each of her index fingers. Her big toenail was bleeding a little and the rainwater spread the blood across the front of her dirty white sandal.

The lights were all out in the house and, as Annie rummaged through her sack of a purse, she checked the windows for signs of life. A glimmer of metal caught her eye and she zeroed in on a single, shiny key in the keyhole of the front door. *That's creepy,* she thought.

She dialed Mike's number and immediately hung up after the first ring. *Ohmygod. I'm an idiot. That was close.* She redialed: Jon.

As it rang, she wondered why someone would leave a single key in a door. Who keeps keys separate from their key rings?

No answer. She didn't want to leave a message—she hated her voice and knew she'd sound frenzied and manic—so she pulled the phone down from her ear and ended the call. *How long was this stupid deluge going to go on? Should she just go home? Or maybe it was a sign. He's six years younger, anyway, and what does he even do for a job?* She should've left Jon a message.

As Annie turned back to the door, she was shocked to see an empty keyhole. No key anywhere. *What?* She stepped back and inspected the floor to see if it had fallen. No key. *Where did it go? Am I imagining this?*

The rain was drumming a foreboding rhythm into the earth and the wind kicked up just enough to say, "Get out of there, Annie."

Still facing the empty keyhole, she slowly backed up and put her phone delicately back into her bag, as if the door were a lion, ready to pounce, and her phone were a weapon. She was showing the cat she meant no harm.

The lion roared; a clap of thunder shook the porch. Annie spun around and sprinted headfirst back into the downpour with the wild animal chasing behind her, nipping at her bloody toes.

3rd September 2012

LINGERING

Before picking up her daughter from Dance Team, Rachel had been quietly listening to the car radio, something she rarely did, focusing on taking slow, deliberate breaths. Her daughter Imani was now in the passenger seat, breaking down who was seeing whom—they don't say "dating" anymore—*Kala was upset with Allie because she had a crush on Henry, even though Kala asked him to see a movie with her and her sisters.*

As she drove, Rachel asked enough pointed questions so Imani could tell she was paying attention like a good mom. But the radio was playing the song from that night by the singer whose name she couldn't remember (or care to) and the lyrics took her back to the second they first kissed, in his car, in front of her apartment building, back in 1997. 1998? It smelled like old French fries in his car and he joked about Wendy's. As the beat dropped and the chorus began, Imani asked, "Where are we going? You passed our street."

The car had been driving itself and Rachel's eyes were blurry. "We did? Oops—I don't know where my head's at!"

She knew exactly where her head was: touching his cheek, moving her fingers across his dark stubble, inhaling his scent—a strong aftershave he wore every day instead of deodorant. The smell still lingered in certain drawers in the bedroom . . .

As they pulled slowly into the driveway, Imani asked if she could ride her bike around the block a little.

From the way "Why not?" stumbled out of Rachel's mouth, Imani knew immediately something was wrong and reached out to touch her hand on the steering wheel. As they made eye contact, Rachel saw his eyes in Imani's and blinked a watery smile.

Imani decided she would surprise her mom and make two boxes of macaroni and cheese so she wouldn't have to cook for her or her older brother—if he came home for dinner from his girlfriend's house. She'd make frozen corn in the microwave and mix up some Crystal Light lemonade and set the table and light the big, center candle and it would be a real family dinner again. Just without Dad.

28th September 2012

FRANCHISE

As his middle school social studies teacher explained the details of the architecture assignment to design a new type of building, Charlie Tekkata came up with a Big Idea: hotels *in* airports. His hyper-detailed ground plan in colored pencil got an A+, along with a note in red pen from Mrs. Pollard that said, "Neat idea. Keep going!" So he did.

Months before graduating *cum laud*e with his undergrad degree in Communications, he applied to five graduate schools to get his MBA. He wisely selected only prestigious, Ivy League graduate schools, so he could network with other high-level entrepreneurs while earning his Masters.

He chose not to continue with school after his mother passed away suddenly and a high-school friend offered him a partnership in a Dunkin' Donuts franchise in his hometown of Trenton, New Jersey. A small business would teach Charlie everything he needed to know about managing people and finances and the market and sales and budgets and overhead and corporate America!

And yet, seven years after their successful grand opening, Charlie Tekkata, self-made thousandaire, woke up from a nightmare; Dunkin' Donuts was not the answer. He immediately drove to his father's home at 4 a.m. and snuck into the attic to rummage through every cardboard box until he found that ground plan from Mrs. Pollard's class.

27th June 2013

BLIND SPOT

Maybe she dropped her cell phone too hard last week as she hurried out of her Camry into the Tanglewood Kroger. Maybe she hadn't updated the settings or done that recommended update from the App Store. Or maybe it just needed to be turned off for a minute. Brittany held down the power button and the screen went black.

She could relate—she knew what it felt like to need a reboot every now and then. Getting her first job at Lush last year and meeting Mel who was actually the one who introduced her to Greg at that party was like the perfect do-over after a really shitty sophomore year. Not the best grades, not the best choices, if you know what I mean. Everything changed when she started at Lush.

How long should she wait before switching it back on? When Brittany was a kid, her older brother Travis would pull their Super Nintendo cartridges out and blow on them, lightly tapping to fifteen on top of the system before restarting it. It had been at least fifteen seconds for sure, so she pressed the power button again to turn the phone back on.

C'mon, c'mon, c'mon . . .

She drove past Botentourt Road. If he didn't text back, she would know something was going on. Ugh! He always texted back. He always picked up the phone. It was a major selling point for making him her boyfriend—he was a communicator. Not like Jake. Or Rob. Rob would rather have done anything else but call her back. He thought "playing it cool" was sexy and that smoking pot all weekend was partying. Obviously, he'd never been to a sorority blowout at Radford. Nor would they ever invite him to one. Jake either. What a dumbass! She knew she had really struck gold when she met Greg. Finally, someone who was her mental and social equal.

Still no text. She went to her favorites and tapped his name (first on the list, just above Mel and Mom). She put the phone on speaker as she made the turn onto the highway. She sped up the ramp and the sound of the revving engine only furthered her desperation to reach him. It was a good thing she was on her way to Mel's. Mel always calmed her down and, as they sat and ate

Doritos or M&M's (her favorite—but not the blue ones), Doctor Mel would dispel her concerns about whatever was plaguing her (usually boy trouble) and help her see the best side of the situation.

No answer. No answer again! She threw her phone into the passenger seat and a white car merged suddenly in front of her from the exit ramp. Her father always told her to mind her blind spots. Even though she ragged on him about using the word "mind" like that, like some old, fussy British grammar professor, she remembered the expression every time she drove. *Mind* your blind spots. She slowed down to allow the car in front of her a safer distance.

Her mother would rather she'd never even got her license. If she'd had her way, Brittany would still be taking the bus to and from high school with all the freshmen and sophomores (and loser juniors). No seniors would be caught dead on the bus. Neither would Brittany.

Greg was probably high. He'd probably gone over to one of his buddies' places and smoked himself into oblivion. Going to his house to look for him would just be a waste of gas and freak his parents out.

"Jesus, I'm totally obsessing," Brittany laughed to herself. She could already hear Mel saying "That loser isn't worth your time, Brit! Seriously, you need a quarterback, or like, a future doctor, or something. Greg's not even that cute." Of course, he was. I mean, Mel liked Latino guys—what did *she* know?

The light above the intersection at Persinger Road was out and she almost missed the turn onto Mel's block. There was no one else on the street, so Brittany spun the wheel and U-turned back towards the dark corner. Maybe Mel's older brother would be home and could fix her phone if it really were shot. He was a complete dork, but he knew his tech.

Brittany rounded the last bend and approached Mel's driveway at the end of the block. In front of the yard was Greg's red Nissan. She knew it was his because one door was a different shade of red.

Brittany's pulse began to race. What the hell is he doing here?! She steered her car right up next to the Nissan to make sure she wasn't hallucinating.

Her phone chimed. Greg: *At a friend's place. Can't talk.*

10th July 2013

VOLCANO

Your birthday sneaks up on you when you're older, especially since the kids all moved out and your husband, Les, passed away. Your social contact is limited to the cashiers at the grocery store and CVS, the tollbooth agents on the turnpike, and solicitor phone calls—all of which you make the best of, trying to be an excellent listener, full of compassion and keen interest. You spend days by yourself without hearing human voices and sometimes think about giving away your televisions. Usually you are glad to have the solace and silence.

Your birthday feels different this year. You wake up and count the days on the calendar, going back through them to confirm that, yes, today is actually the 11th of March. You grumble "sixty-nine" out loud. You take a deep breath, and, in place of a sigh, you groan out a frustrated, ferocious volcano of an explosion that releases a deep sadness, and your knees half-buckle and you have to sit down. Once you've sat, you take a shallow breath and whisper "seventy."

You feel the familiar urge to light something on fire. So you find all the lighters and matches in the house and put them in a big soup pot and fill it with water so you can't burn it down.

24th July 2013

THEO

Anya wasn't there when he got home from Chinatown, his secret trip to Daredevil Tattoos. She wasn't at work at the café on Delancey, either. He sent her two texts after reaching her voicemail, quickly spouting off "hey" then "where r u?"

He wandered back home through the Lower East Side, grinning to himself. He couldn't wait for her to see it.

"i thought u were gonna be home with me tonight. i got something to show u."

Twenty minutes later, he sent "helllloooo??"

Then "fine i'll just make myself dinner."

Anya wasn't there when he woke up sweaty at 3 a.m., still drunk on their hot couch, to the sounds of two guys arguing in Spanish out on the corner. He slammed the window shut and checked his phone for a sign that she was still alive.

His skin was more tender than he expected, considering it was his bicep, albeit the underside. He cleaned it off under the kitchen faucet, above his bowl of cereal, the cold water both soothing and stinging like a bitch. He stared at it, her name in raised purple-black cursive. The "y" was bigger than the other letters.

Theo had once thrown a television out a window. It was the most brash, violent, impulsive thing he'd done up until that afternoon.

The skin around Anya's name was lobster red, the color of a child's first sunburn, and his whole arm started to quiver as he held it up under the countertop light, inspecting it. He could see his heart beating through the veins below her name.

Hearing Anya's distinct chunky heels on the stairs in the hallway, Theo shut off the faucet and hurried back to the couch, taking a moment to decide which way he should lie so her name was right-side up when his arm was poised overhead. He plopped down facing the door, pushing the pillows back to maximize his sprawl and drew his oily hair back away from his face so she could see his sweet, satisfied expression as he dozed. He inhaled deeply, trying to force himself back into long, luxurious sleep breaths. A door opened and shut across the hall. It wasn't Anya.

Fuck her. After this massive, amazing, over-the-top, generous gesture of passion and commitment, the perfect antidote to their fight last week, the ultimate show of dedication, she disappears? What kind of emotional warfare was this?

Last Tuesday, Theo caught Anya looking at the bartender at Two Bits and clocked her hunger. She denied it, told him to back off, heel, sit. Her excuses were delivered with outrageous intensity and their conversation about having an open relationship came rolling back up again. Why was she so upset about him not wanting kids if she was just gonna go whore off with whomever? Who was more committed here?

The thought of her sitting in the back of some bar right now with a random hipster shithead, kissing his stubble and chewing on his ear, lit something inside of Theo and he jumped up, lunging towards her computer on the corner desk. It had a picture of the two of them floating around on the screensaver, their coy smiles bouncing against the sides in a dizzying rhythm. He pulled the laptop off of the desk and lifted it high above his head, bending backwards and stretching the skin around the tattoo so the scabs tore open a little. He let out a throaty growl as he threw Anya's stupid face as hard as he could into the brick wall.

~

It didn't matter which Anya saw first—the wreckage of computer parts strewn around the living room or her name boldly etched into Theo's armpit—they both said the same thing to her in her mother's voice.

She tiptoed to the drawer by the closet, found her passport and envelope of tip money, zipped them into her backpack, and took extra care to close the front door quietly enough not to wake him.

14th October 2013

THE CINDY

The first droplet hit Tom's left wrist, just above his watch, waking him up with a jolt. He inspected it with dismay. Of course it was raining. His birthday was cursed; it had rained every year for as long as he could remember.

Somehow it was already 4:02. While he was napping, the beautiful sunny day had turned sour, the dirty grey clouds rolling over themselves toward the boat. Another drop fell onto his forehead and another against the glass window behind him.

Tom began yanking in the nets. "Fuck," he muttered. They should've stopped at 2:00 and turned back, but Dale had been drinking and they hadn't caught many fish, so they decided to go another hour or so. "It's starting!" he shouted loud enough for Dale to hear.

As he dragged the heavy, wet ropes up and over his legs, the rain started tapping the basin around him until it was a steady pour. Tom clenched his jaw tightly. It was gonna be a rocky, stormy ride back to the harbor and he'd be wet and late and tired as hell and he wasn't gonna have time to swing by to see his girlfriend and he'd have to go straight home. His mom was making a birthday fish fry.

The rain was coming down in earnest now and the clouds were turning almost purple, expanding, and widening. Where was Dale? If he was passed out drunk, there was no way in hell Tom could wake him up. When Dale fell asleep on the table at the Wharf Pub, they just left him there. Marla, the no-nonsense bartender with a heavy Massachusetts burr (and heavier hips), tried shaking him, but with a guy that big—and that blitzed—they all knew there was no chance.

"And a crappy haul!" Tom tied off the net, which had maybe a dozen measly tuna and a stray plastic bottle. He walked portside to check the front for the old drunk, his feet already starting to slosh in his drenched shoes.

A clap of thunder shoved Tom against the side of the boat and a massive strike of lightning across the sky was like an unzipping of the cloud above him. The downpour was intense, and he was blinded by the onslaught. He jumped into the control room and shouted Dale's name. Where was that drunk fucker?!

Tom had only a few years of experience with this size rig and wasn't confident with the older navigation equipment. The thought of steering her home in this type of storm made the blue vein in the left side of his neck pound. He peeked over the front window and expected to see a limp barrel of a man zonked out on the bow, clutching his Jim Beam, but there wasn't a sign of Captain Dale. The wind was picking up and a sudden burst of rain pelted the door next to Tom.

"Tom can't do anything on his own! He's an idiot!"

When he was a boy scout, Tom used to cheat off of his cousin Nicky. One afternoon, while attempting to earn a sewing badge, he watched Nicky carefully thread his needle and expertly stitch a striped yellow swatch of cotton onto a blue flannel shirt. The thread was a crisp white, and he stood in awe as Nicky's thin fingers moved in rhythm along the side of his colorful quilt. How did he know how to do that? He turned to his manual, which must've been three hundred years old, to search for the "Sewing & Mending" chapter, wondering what he had missed. He wanted to hand off his pieces to Nicky, along with his two cookies, but he knew he couldn't bribe him anymore.

Nicky had a sad-faced fragility to him. Because of his unpopularity at school, he was determined to be the best at everything scouting, a social fresh start. Other boys' attention spurred him to share his successes with them which made him a total pushover in Tom's eyes. Nicky saved the day every time: Pinewood Derby, Father-Son Bake-Off, Mask Making. During the recent tent-pitching competition, though, they got caught by the Scout Leader, who just happened to be Nicky's dad. He grabbed Nicky as he was writing the sequence on Tom's inner wrist with a Sharpie. Nicky cried and begged his dad to let Tom participate in the challenge so he could earn his Tent Badge, too, but rules are rules. "No cheaters allowed."

Nicky looked up from his sewing and whispered to Tom, "I can't help you anymore. You have to do it yourself." That wasn't what Tom wanted to hear and he yanked Nicky's quilt from his hands and ripped out the needle and thread. Not surprisingly, Nicky began crying instantly and with fervor. He pointed his finger at Tom's face and turned his wails towards his father, the Arbiter. Tom groaned and crossed his arms in defiance, expecting to defend himself for being a bully. But Nicky wasn't only a crybaby, it turned out. He was also a self-righteous prick.

"Tom can't do anything on his own! He stole my sewing! He always steals because I do everything right and he's an idiot!"

Even though he hadn't thought about it in years, it was Nicky's voice that Tom heard on that boat in the driving rain when he realized Dale had probably fallen overboard and he was going to have to get himself and this ship home safely in a storm on his nineteenth birthday.

"Tom can't do anything on his own!" Fucking Nicky. "Tom can't do anything on his own!" Nicky's voice bounced around the control room as the boat swayed left, then sharply right. Tom's heart was pounding and, between the anxious thumps and the hurricane drumming against the hollow hull, he could hardly think. His fingertips hovered over the controls. His eyes darted from the odometer to the compass to the ship log to the steering wheel to the storm outside, which was now impossible to see through.

"This is when your survival instincts are supposed to kick in, you idiot." Tom could see his fingers shaking.

Another clap of monstrous thunder broke him from his panic and a thought occurred to him. What if Dale is locked downstairs? Maybe he slipped and fell going to the bathroom? If he was down somewhere in the cabin nursing a bloody head gash, Tom had to rescue him so that he could steer them home safely. It was the only way they were both going to survive.

Tom took a breath and shoved the door open into the gale-force winds and threw himself towards the galley. Rain came in from every direction—even up, somehow—and Tom collapsed to his knees in front of the door handle in the deck, grabbing the sides to steady himself. He squinted through the downpour, streams of water flowing down his face. With one big heave-ho, he had the hatch up, and he dove headfirst down the steep ladder. His hands slammed against the wooden deck hard, and the door above him banged shut with a thud.

The quiet was sudden and unnerving. "DALE," Tom shouted. He stood up and wiggled his left wrist, which throbbed. "OW, my goddamned hand broke. Dale? You broke my fucking wrist!" No answer.

The bathroom door was ajar, swaying open and shut with the rocking of the boat. Dale wasn't in there. The main room was dark and as Tom stepped in, he reached hesitantly for the light switch, afraid of what gruesome scene might be revealed.

"Dale?" He steadied himself in the doorway with both knees bent and flipped the light on.

On the floor of the otherwise empty room were Dale's boots, coveralls, t-shirt, hat, and underwear, neatly laid out on top of one another, as if he had been abducted by aliens and his clothes were all that were left.

~

"No, Mother!"

Cynthia knew how much she hated being called Mother.

"I'm done. This time I'm really done. I can't even count how many chances we've given it. My body is screaming at the top of its lungs at me and this time, I'm listening. . . . I'll tell him tonight. . . . What? I don't know. We've—we've just talked it all to death and I can't bear another pleading argument with him. I'm out of tears and ideas, and I've hit a wall. Like, a totally new level of wall. . . . That's the thing! I don't *know* what he wants anymore! He doesn't want anything. He's gotten so fat—you should see him."

Cynthia briskly rounded the corner of the last kiosk in the mall where a very relaxed salesgirl was texting on her sparkly pink Blackberry. On cue, the girl looked up and smiled, blithely holding up four fingers at Cynthia, their unspoken routine. She nodded back and continued at a quick pace into her fifth lap, using her arms to propel her forward as she speed-walked.

"Like obese fat. Sad, sickly, has-a-waddle-and-needs-new-clothes-that-we-can't-afford fat. . . . Of course I've tried to help him with it! Geez. This is the problem! I've been desperately trying to keep us afloat—all by myself. I can only make so many healthy meals and invite him on my walks so many times. He has got to start making *himself* healthy and happy. That's what I'm going to do. On my own! I know it won't be easy to start over, but I'm gonna do it. . . . Well, I work with all sorts of incredible men at work. I've been asked on dates. . . . Yes, I have! Last year, a supplier from up the coast, or Dover, or somewhere. He was real cute, too. . . . No, I didn't *Get His Number*, I'm married. I mean, I was married then. I was not thinking about other men like that. Actually, I think that was when I thought I was finally pregnant from that last in vitro attempt."

A janitor stepped out from a doorway a few feet ahead of Cynthia and quickly jumped back against the wall out of her path.

"Yeah, so, sorry—Excuse me!—sorry. Yeah, I thought I was pregnant, so I wasn't going to go and try to hook up with the hot medical supplies guy. Anyway, my point. My point is I only have a couple years left—tick, tock—and Dale and I have been doomed for years . . . yes, DOOMED. And I feel close to crying just thinking about what a waste of time it's all been."

Cynthia slowed her gait as she approached Nordstrom's and took longer steps. Half a lap to go. Cool down.

"So, it's happening tonight, Mother."

She thought of Dale, sitting there in front of the goddamned television—which *she* bought them—watching some stupid show, staring at it like a zombie, with his feet up on the coffee table—which *her* parents gave them—with his belly showing. "Hey, honey," he'd say, "how was work?" in that tone that meant "Oh, you're home already? Keep it down, TV's on." He'd be drinking, naturally, and she would stomp in, grab his bottle and remote in a flash, and stand between the blob and the boob tube.

"It's OVER," she'd shout. "You got what you wanted, Dale. You ruined everything and I'm finally leaving." She wouldn't cry. She was a warrior princess burning down the village. "I'm taking everything with me—the cat, the bed, the TV, my car, my blender, my fucking dignity! But you can keep this." She'd yank off her cheap gold band and hurtle it between his eyes. "I'm going to go find a man who loves me and wants to have a family with me—and *can* have a family with me. And he'll take care of himself and love me and won't smell like goddamn fish."

Then, of course, he'd say no, no, no, that he loves her, and he only smelled like fish because he bought the boat for her. And that he wanted more than anything to give her a child if he could. And that he couldn't help his weight, he was sick, and he understood why she'd want to leave. He was a piece of shit, and she deserved better. And she'd hold her head high and try not to look at him, but in avoiding his eyes, she'd end up seeing their wedding picture on the beat-up credenza: Young Cynthia and Young Dale ecstatic in love, gripping each other on the deck of *The Cindy,* his new pride and joy.

She'd cry. And she wouldn't be able to stop. Because he wasn't the reason their marriage was a mess. And he couldn't control his weight. And she couldn't help him. And he tried so hard for years to make her happy, but it was never enough. And he didn't even want to be a fisherman, but he knew she loved the ocean. And it was so sweet when she found that book on sailing the first year they were dating because he'd been in school to be a mechanic, but she was getting her degree in marine biology and her father had been a captain of a yacht. And he couldn't control the terrible decline in the Delaware fishing industry in the late 90's, or the fact that his sperm count was indescribably low, or the fact that they were both just really unhappy people, living really unhappy lives. He'd probably start crying too, and she'd look at him and feel flush with regret, sick to her stomach for being such a heartless bitch to the boy who had once pledged that he'd do anything to make her love him. They would embrace on the couch and mourn the unspecial life they built together and then go to bed quietly, feeling the cosmic apology they owed each other.

"Hold on, Mom. Hold on."

Cynthia reached the last kiosk again, where the salesgirl was waiting for their high-five with one hand up. Cynthia slapped it triumphantly and the girl said, "You totally killed it today," in a cheerful, yet somewhat mocking tone.

"Thanks! See you tomorrow—or something," Cynthia replied in an exasperated way, which she felt was more teenage vernacular than her own. She took her hand off of the phone speaker and put it back to her ear as she hustled to the parking lot.

"I should go. I need to pick up something for dinner on the way home. . . . Okay. . . . Love you, Mom. . . . Yes, yes, of course I'll call you later."

~

Dale let his gaze slowly fall down his bare chest, past his dark red neck and his white, veiny breasts—they were breasts now, with their hairy, wide nipples that looked like sad, saggy eyes—to his enormous stomach. It looked like

Santa's, no longer just pudgy or plump, but a whole bowl full of jelly. It wasn't jolly, though. It wasn't Santa. He was gigantic. He had become a whale, Cindy's favorite animal.

He took both sides and shook his gut up and down. He could feel his genitals jiggle, but couldn't see them in the mirror. In fact, he couldn't remember the last time he actually took a good, hard look at the revolting tub of a body in the mirror before him. He was disgusting. He was trash. He was compost. An old, beaten-up, tired version of himself filled with helium and expanded beyond comprehension.

Where was his Jim? He looked under the shelf for another bottle. One left. He twisted the top off and threw it on top of his clothes which were in a pile next to him. He swallowed gulp after gulp, tipping the Jim back so it made that *glug, glug, glug* sound as it slid down his throat. He couldn't even really taste it anymore.

His coveralls were massive, and Dale kneeled on the floor to see exactly how wide they were. He pulled the legs right-side out and spread the waist wide. God, he was fat. He laid the hat down above and set the boots below. He was making a melted snowman.

"Hah," he thought, "A snow angel named Dale." He chuckled to himself and took another deep swig of whiskey.

"That's me. A flat, stupid version of me."

Cindy deserved better. Hell, he deserved better, but, ah well.

Another gulp.

He stood back up to address the mirror. There he was. This was it. All these years. This is what everything led to. How did it even happen? When did this belly start growing? When did everything go to shit? Was it the fight about the car? Was it because he never took out the trash when he said he would? Was it her cancer scare? Was it her affair with a high school boyfriend? Was it his flirting with Marla? Was it his ugly penis? Was it because he never took her to Europe? Was it because he hated her dad? Was it just not meant to be? Was it all a mistake? Did he miss the signs? Did he pick the wrong girl? Or did he make all the right choices and then just fuck them up? If he could do it all over, would he have been able to save it? Who cares. This is what it is now, right?

He sucked down the last of the bottle, set it on the shelf, and started up the ladder.

It was brighter outside than he anticipated, and the afternoon sun felt good on the translucent skin around his middle. He became very aware of exactly how naked he was and how far from shore they were. It was freer than he'd ever felt.

Dale squinted through the glaring light, looking towards the back of the boat for the kid to make sure he wasn't watching. He stepped to the railing and looked out at the horizon. He half expected a whale to breach, calling for him to join in.

A storm was approaching in the distance and a slight wind was picking up. He leaned his weight to the right and took a step over the rail with his left leg, the hot metal bars searing the back of his calf and thigh.

Another check back for the kid—he didn't want him to catch him.

This was for Cindy. This was for PawPaw. This was for all the people who told him he was going places. Or was smart. Or cool or funny or handsome. You were all wrong. I'm a fucking whale.

He took a shallow breath in and a careful leap out, falling into the icy water with a heavy splash.

The ocean was freezing. His chest was tight with shock as he paddled furiously down to below the ship, where his fingers scrambled to pull him underneath the bow. Dale blinked open his eyes underwater. Through the dark, salty water below him he saw two gigantic blue whales, staring up with sympathetic, black eyes. They whined a deep, loving whale call.

"Hello," one bellowed.

"Hello, Dale," groaned the other.

"Don't be afraid. Let go."

"Come home."

Dale tilted down towards them and pushed off against the bottom of the boat. As he swam deeper, drifting lower and lower into the darkness, he called to the whales, his brothers. "I know your sadness," he gurbled, and the last of his bubbles floated up towards *The Cindy*.

PART THREE
–
HAIKU

1.

every grain of sand
settles onto the right beach
at the perfect time.

> 23rd November 2011

2.

Maple stood there, tall,
proud of her plot and the
space she filled with her

wide, majestic arms,
upturned leaf hands, and broad trunk
leaning to one side.

Pushing up out of
the backyard and reaching high,
she never wavered,

like an abused spouse
willing to endure years of
neglect and weather.

"When I die someday,
hopefully they'll miss me and
realize my worth.

Then there won't be shade
or songbirds near their windows,
and they'll miss my leaves—

soft green in the spring,
golden in September, then
blazing orange-red."

"Fat chance," said the bush,
"They've wanted you gone for years.
You just block their view.

They rake and they moan
and they can't plant much else; you
take up the garden."

The tree's branches sagged.
"So why, then, was I put here?"
Her leaves felt heavy.

"You were already
here when I arrived, so I
have no idea."

Maple pondered this.
She wasn't anyone's tree.
This was her land first.

"They can cut me down,
they can turn me to flooring
or carve me right up,

they can forget I
was ever here, but I know—
I was a great tree."

30th July 2012

3.

sip my words slowly,
i would hate to see you choke
on my opinions.

2nd March 2003

4.

knowing she'll be late,
she wonders about even
going in to work.

sometimes in that beat
right before leaving the house,
she spits in the sink,

then looks up into
the mirror, checks her lipstick,
and shakes her head no—

"i look terrible
and i need new mascara,"
squinting at herself.

it wasn't just the
makeup she disapproved of;
she looked like her mom.

she has this routine
every morning; "bet they
won't even miss me."

9th February 2006

5.

on a grassy square—
a proud stance silhouetted,
a gentle look down

from the falling sun
admiring his strong back,
but i found him first.

28th February 2006

6.

you are a guitar,
a striking instrument i've
never learned to strum,

something i always
imagined i'd play someday,
and now i have to

learn all the right chords.

2nd March 2006

7.

the space you gave me
and the warmth that you've let off
i have moved into.

15th April 2006

8.

you might as well be
in one of the Dakotas,
quietly buried.

21st July 2006

9.

peaches become ripe
when they are ready—not when
you want to eat them.

27th July 2006

10.

a single finger
cannot pick up a pencil
without assistance.

bound together by
stasis and status, they take
baby steps *en masse.*

safety in numbers
protects crucial kinfolk who
can't fend for themselves.

> 20th August 2006

11.

> sanctify a touch
> and you start a ball rolling.
> where does this hill go?

>> 9th September 2006

12.

mother calmly sits
with chin raised and wide eyes,
a woman waiting.

cooling both her heels,
choosing to let the clock tick
instead of clucking.

when she's not talking,
her staunch message is strongest:
subtle punishment.

> 11th April 2008

13.

sometimes when you feel
the happiest, you are the
most vulnerable.

> 29th June 2008

14.

the rhumba rhythms
and late-night box truck rumbles
are now soothing sounds.

> 23rd July 2008

15.

whipped and flung sideways,
trod upon and left to die,
this insipid weed

sets its roots back in,
proudly returning to choke
the cultivated.

1st September 2008

16.

a tree grips tightly
to its branches through the gusts,
its leaves do not care.

26th September 2008

17.

time has changed nothing
except the mediocre
clothes he likes to wear.

11th October 2008

18.

who are you? who now?
impatiently stepping off
another high ledge?

caught floating between
frozen, numbing apathy
and passionate winds?

        10th November 2009

19.

        stopped along the walk
        to let myself truly see
        the breadth of autumn.

                3rd December 2009

20.

it doesn't take much
to make children happier,
just throw them around.

        6th July 2011

HOSPICE

She's a strong fighter,
but this, this is not how she
wants to be living.

Sitting, waiting, still—
one lung gone, full of fluid,
the other drowning.

She's speaking softly
of flowers, cards, simple meals,
Jamaican nurses.

She's aging quickly;
last month she looked seventy,
now she looks her age.

A soft sadness sits
like a thin dust layer on
every surface.

The gentle scent of
inevitability,
closing its circle.

7th July 2011

BLESSING FOR YOUR TRIP

(for Artie)

May the tide that drew you in
to each of our lives
in surprising moments of serendipity
take you back to where you began safely.
We will be waiting here, sharing little plates
on the sand we used to share with you,
blanketed together, anxious
for a sign that you've made it.

May the same undertow
that yanked you out of our view
carry you swiftly to some peaceful shore,
maneuvering around the currents of loss,
beyond the miserable whirlpooling eddies of grief,
safely back home.

May you laugh when you arrive
at the ridiculousness of it all
and, when we finally hear that joyful roar,
we'll pack our little plates
and we, too, will head home.

10th May 2020

GRATITUDE

This book would not be in your hands if it weren't for some incredibly talented people—a beautiful hive of loved ones who inspire me, lift me up, keep me grounded, and offer me unconditional love, care, guidance, support, laughter, or (in most cases) all of the above:

Ellen Kurcis, Judy Mayeux, and Constantina Boudouvas for joyfully introducing me to creative writing and emboldening me to become a writer.

Angela Kiessel and Michelle Fletcher, each a proofreading powerhouse and beloved Scribner sibling.

Lindsey Heddleston Smith for your inspiring illustrations and the gentle beauty and clarity you bring to everything you touch.

Kallie Falandays and Tell Tell Poetry for your expert care as this book took shape.

Bryan Bradford and Dustin Layton for believing in me and urging my writing forward.

Paul Benjamins and the other souls who support me from beyond, including my grandparents William & Helen, Del & Geneva, Sidney, and Bob & Doris.

The wonderful community of Broadway stage managers I call my friends: Matt (and Pamela), Sarah Elaine, MK, Jo, Kenny, Anne, Heather, Laurie, Katie, Claudia, Adam, Martha, Shelley, David, Sara, Andrea, Francesca, Jamie, Rachel, Lee, Jeff, Andrew, Pam, Josh, Kaitlyn, and Artie.

My loving friends and kindred spirits: Gracy, Jody, Julia, Naomi, Danny, Jenn, André, Michael & Andy, Sweet Ben, Becky, Merle, Marcus, Todd, Cassondra, Maia, Juliet, Roopan, Danielle, Emily Daniel, and my chosen family—Heather & Matty, Jodi, Collin, Mikey, Jesse, Adam, and Kyle & Thor.

My extended family: Linh, Lili, Gabe, Andrew, Jules, Aurora, my godson Walden Leif, my godmother Carroll, my fairy godmothers Jeri & Kyra, Jonathan, Meg & Will, Jaqui, Arthur, JohnHenry, Annie & Paul, Joe & Norma, Randy & Shelby, Mardi & David, Devon, Jennifer, Patrick, Ruth, David & Martha, Matt & Marlita, Dan & Connie, Sarah, Devon, Dick & Cindy, Danielle, Laura, and card shark in-training Geoff.

My parents: Mom, I am so grateful for your love, care, and creativity, your vulnerability, and for always being a spiritual guiding light in my life. Dad, thank you for introducing me to diplomacy, determination, equanimity, and (unwittingly) The Indigo Girls. Holly, thank you for showing me the importance of healthy boundaries, the power of teaching, and card games. Your unconditional love and support mean everything to me.

And lastly, my holy trinity: my best friend and partner-in-crime, Sarita; my incredible brother, Garen; and my love, Ben. I am so fortunate to share this lifetime with you.

JUSTIN SCRIBNER is an author, poet, playwright, producer, teacher, and stage manager. His short plays include *john/paul, Commuters Muted,* and *Saeedeh & Nasha* and he co-wrote the musical *A Host of Sparrows* with Sarita Louise Rhodes. Justin has stage managed thirteen Broadway plays and musicals, including the Tony-winning revival of *Once On This Island* and the long-running shows *Rock of Ages, A Chorus Line,* and *RENT*. This is his first collection of poetry and short stories.

justinscribner.com

www.ingramcontent.com/pod-product-compliance
Lightning Source LLC
Chambersburg PA
CBHW062027290426
44108CB00025B/2808